THE D.C. DIALECT:
How to Master
The New Language
of Washington
In Ten Easy Lessons

One criminal act for which the evidence is overwhelming is what Watergate has done to the language. It's as if everybody in Washington learned English from Lewis Carroll's Humpty Dumpty, who said: "When I use a word, it means just what I choose it to mean. The question is: Which is to be master? That's all!" And the rest of us are left feeling like Alice in "Through A Looking Glass"—protesting she can't believe in impossible things, and being told she just hasn't had enough practice.

Walter Cronkite
CBS Radio Network News
July 11, 1974

THE D.C. DIALECT:

*How To Master
The New Language
of Washington
In Ten Easy Lessons*

by
Paul Morgan
and
Sue Scott

WASHINGTON MEWS BOOKS
A Division of New York University Press
1975

If my answers sound confusing, I think they are confusing because the questions are confusing, and the situation is confusing and I'm not in a position to clarify it.

Ron Ziegler

Preface

By THEODORE M. BERNSTEIN

As if the English language hadn't been taking a sufficient battering from Madison Avenue, Washington officialdom has now gotten into the act too. The text that follows shows how. It goes further and instructs you in how to cultivate the proper sloppiness that will allow you to make your way in Washington circles and even in the Oval Room. It tells you how to be obscure, pompous, awkward and incorrect in your speech.

The study is not easy to master. When you want to say that something won't work, you won't think, unless you have done some cramming, of using the word "counter-productive." If you want to explain that something will remain as is, you might not be able to come up with "zero growth." Or if you want to avoid the nasty word "ration-ing," it might not occur to you to say "end-use allocation." Those words do not appear in the present manual, but the method and plenty of examples do.

As the authors suggest, one underlying cause of the dialect is the prevalence of lawyers on the District of Columbia scene. Lawyers always avoid saying things too sharply, lest they leave loopholes or commit themselves. On top of that, the opening of Watergate loosed a flood of evasiveness, a need for secretiveness and fear of perjury. The result, as the authors say, was an arcane language. And the people in the capital make it, if you will pardon the Biblical allusion, as arcane as they are able.

The examples cited in this book make the important point that the official dialect these days is a mumbled jumble, sometimes unintentionally obscure but often intentionally deceptive. How much it will spread and how long it will last is anybody's guess. We can hope that it will not persist beyond the next dia-election.

Meanwhile, have fun with "The D.C. Dialect."

Mr. Bernstein is Consulting Editor of The New York Times and author of the Careful Writer *and other books on English usage.*

Table of Contents

Chapter One

At This Particular Point
in Time

*I ran into Mr. Liddy. He was essentially heading down
the hall.*

HUGH W. SLOAN, JR.

How would you like to:

1. Become an Infamous Personality overnight?
2. Be the focal point of a nationally publicized trial?
3. Write an "inside" book about your career in Washington and make a lot of money?
4. Write a "confession" book about your career in Washington and make a lot of money?
5. Be able to understand "inside" and "confession" books about careers in Washington?
6. Rest and relax for a few months in a Country Club Jail?

1

7. Climb the corporate ladder of success?
8. Pass as a lawyer?

Well, you can do all these things and more! All you have to do is learn the new language of Washington, which we will help you do in just ten easy lessons. As soon as you learn the official speech of the high and mighty, of people in authority, of the insiders in our nation's capital, all these advantages can be yours. Never again will you have to languish in obscurity, eke out a boring living, scratch to make ends meet. If you will take the time to learn this powerful new speech, there's no limit to how far you can go!

People who speak plain old English, at least in the nation's capital, are simply out of step—are listening to the beat of the wrong drum, so to speak. At this particular point in time, Washington politicians no longer speak the language of our forefathers, which is just as well, all things considered. After all, times have changed from the days of the Gettysburg Address and the Declaration of Independence; Washington today is a far cry from the Washington of Washington. And since politicians have always been in the forefront of change, they have been among the first to recognize the need to match the *sound* with the *sense* of today, as it were. Nowadays, the new language of politics can be heard on the lips of all the *smart* people in D.C.

The new language of Washington has been called various names—Washingtonspeak, Doublespeak, Newspeak, etc.—but most people think of it as the language of Watergate, because that episode revealed for the first time just how widespread and influential this speech had become. We prefer to call the language the D.C. Dialect, however, partly because it originated in Washington, D.C., partly because it predates Watergate, but mostly because it transcends Watergate and is used by virtually all congressmen, senators, administration officials, and, to a lesser extent, by corporation executives, computer systems designers and others. As students of language, we have been following the evolution of this dialect for several years with mounting excitement, realizing it to be one of the most original forms of speech of our century. In fact, we go so far as to predict that in the very near future the entire nation will be emulating the Very Important People who now speak the D.C. Dialect!

The VIPs who speak this new dialect accomplish wonders with it. Through the sheer power of rhetoric, officials and politicians can lie to the nation and be blameless simply by labeling their lies "inoperative"; they can perform undemocratic and unconstitutional acts in the name of "national security"; they can bomb underdeveloped countries with no one the wiser by calling the bombings "protective reaction strikes"; they can manipulate the export market in the name of "furthering détente"; they can send spies to intervene in the internal affairs of other countries and make such action appear beneficial by naming it "destabilization"; and they can whisk recessions right out of existence by suggesting that the economy is merely suffering from "a lateral waffle."

The vast benefits of such a speech should be obvious: speakers of the dialect can swindle their friends, confound their enemies, and diddle the public with impunity. Clearly, the dialect is one of those exciting products of Yankee ingenuity—the sort of thing Americans come up with when traditional methods don't work—a true product of pragmatism at its best. So weep not for the death of English in high places; the D.C. Dialect is persuasive, pervasive, and slick as owl shit. In short, it is the perfect language for people in authority.

But believe it or not, in the face of overwhelming proof of the superiority of this new language, there are actually people who won't accept it and even people who attack it! Many writers, journalists, assorted English teachers, and even a few nationally known TV commentators have protested these changes in the language. These self-styled purists insist that the English language is being mauled and mangled in our nation's capital, and, indeed, in every corner of the country. These guardians of English claim that politicians are influencing innocent children and suggestible adults to speak a substandard form of the mother tongue. National watchdog committees have even been formed to protect us all from this "language pollution." "Unless we clean up English," the strident voices cry, "we shall soon be a nation of mumbling idiots!"

Nonsense! The critics of the D.C. Dialect are really just a bunch of elitist snobs who think that only educated people should tell us how to speak. Such an undemocratic idea not only flies in the very teeth of the American way, which says that every one of us has the right to speak any way he pleases, but it's downright subversive! We believe the common man will be quick to see that this new language can be his ticket to power, influence and upward job mobility, and any language that can do that has got to be good! We're confident that the man in the street will tell this handful of purists to leave language alone and go back to their own business (whatever *that* is). As James St. Clair so aptly states, "Squabbling over words is not a fruitful exercise."

As the "traditionalist" critics ought to know, Language is the Key to Success, and we believe so strongly in the future of this new speech that we have written this book to teach *you*, the layman, how to master the D.C. Dialect (or DCD for short). We've put the rules of the dialect in the ten easy-to-learn lessons, and all you have to do is just practice a few hours a day and soon you will be a master. Then just watch your life change! High-powered jobs may open for you in Washington, and you may even be asked to run for Congress—or join the White House staff. And you don't even have to move to Washington if you don't want to. You can learn this language right in your own home, and as soon as you master it you're sure to be offered a cozy post in local or state government at the very least, or a management job in a top corporation or ad agency.

Before you plunge into this fascinating and exotic language, however, one word of caution. Not everyone can learn it! If you are elderly, female, or sensitive to language, you may never be able to speak the dialect with any degree of fluency. Senator Ervin is a case in point. Even after several months of exposure to DCD, several hours a day, five days a week during the Watergate hearings, he still speaks English, which goes to prove that you can't teach old senators new speech. Of course the Senator was educated in the days when literature, poetry, the Bible, grammar, history, and other irrelevant subjects were still considered fit courses of study, and his speech habits were evidently permanently affected. A real DCD speaker wouldn't be caught dead quoting the King James version—much less poetry or drama!

If you're a woman, you'd best plan to take up some other line of work and give up ambitions of high-ranking government jobs. We have yet to discover any woman who speaks the dialect with any degree of fluency, which leads us to the conclusion that women have no natural affinity for it. The two high-ranking women in government today speak a substandard form of DCD, and the total absence of women indicted in connection with the Watergate affair further bears out our belief.

As for those of you who are sensitive to language, there

is little we can tell you. You simply haven't the stomach to learn the dialect, and that's all there is to it. You might try drowning your disappointment in an unexpurgated copy of *Paradise Lost*—or a butt of malmsey, whichever is handier. But whatever you do, do *not* listen to our public officials or read their press releases. Too much DCD can destroy a sensitive soul. Like the ladies, you will simply have to resign yourselves to being Very Unimportant Persons.

But for those of you who can take it, here is the definitive book on the most successful speech of our time. Your opportunities are unlimited!

Chapter Two

The D.C. Dialect in
Ten Easy Lessons

Frankly, I'm a human being.
BERNARD L. BARKER

In order to make these lessons in DCD as authentic as possible, we have gone to the master speakers of the dialect so you can learn this language right from the horses'—*mouths,* so to speak. We've gathered examples of DCD from all the important people in Washington, past and present, from the Watergate hearings to press releases to public speeches to the White House Transcripts to public trials. We've left no stone unturned.

In the course of our extensive research, we've made some startling discoveries about the speech and the speechees. Those who hold middle- to high-ranking positions in the federal government speak the pure form of the dialect, and those in low-level jobs exhibit only a bastardized usage. Naturally, lawyers in the District of Columbia speak the purest form of DCD, since they hold 90 per cent of the top positions in government. To these legal worthies, the D.C. Dialect is the logical outgrowth of their natural lawyer talk, known as "legalese."

Lawyers are not the only professional people who have contributed to the evolution of the dialect, however; there are three other major sources: the military, business (advertising in particular), and sports. These four language currents have doubtless been creeping into the speech of authorities for some time, but the rise of DCD coincides, oddly enough, with the election of Richard Nixon as President. We can only speculate on the reasons for this coincidence, but one reason must be the amazing increase in the number of lawyers in Washington from 1968 on. It was about this time that a migration of sorts took place, as hundreds of writers, artists, entertainers, scholars, scientists, and chefs moved out of the capital. Fortunately, businessmen, athletes, and militarists joined the lawyers in the city, and this combination of professions merged, bringing together in one place all those influences that produced the D.C. Dialect. But whatever the underlying reasons for the merger, the happy result is the strong, masculine speech which dominates our capital today.

So here they are—the rules for learning the D.C. Dialect. When you learn them you will be able to at least *pass* for a Washington official. If, however, you should forget your DCD and lapse into English, you will be exposed as an impostor, and all your dreams of glory will be shattered.

Lesson 1:

Be Impersonal

I was asked to disburse to an individual in Los Angeles...

HERBERT W. KALMBACH

The first thing to learn about the D.C. Dialect is that you must cultivate an impersonal tone in your speech lest you be suspected of harboring warm, personal feelings. People who speak DCD set great store on being "cool," which means they do not show their emotions—or have none—it is not quite clear which. Washington officials like to remove themselves from the ordinary concerns of ordinary men, and one of the ways they do this is by being impersonal, which gives them an appearance of aloofness. So begin by pretending you don't know anyone in the world well enough to call him by his first name. You may call him "Mr." So-and-So, but never refer to him casually. All your friends and colleagues are Very Important People, concerned with Lofty Affairs; therefore, you mustn't reduce their status nor suggest warm friendships by referring to them informally.

10

Never refer to people as "people," to men as "men," or to anyone by name unless it is absolutely necessary. Note the use of the word "individual" in the following examples:

He received a call from a male individual in Los Angeles.

JAMES W. MCCORD, JR.

Shortly after midnight, McCord was called by an unidentified individual.

JOHN CAULFIELD

. . . any proper individual.

ROBERT MARDIAN

I've been charged with a highly sensitive mission by the White House to visit and elicit information from an individual whose ideology we aren't entirely sure of.

Transcript of taped conversation between E. HOWARD HUNT and GEN. ROBERT E. CUSHMAN

It is not my purpose to testify for or against any individual.

HERBERT KALMBACH

11

I described this individual in the field.

GORDON STRACHAN

You can learn a lot about this technique by studying the words of General Haig, as he is particularly good at it. Instead of calling Senator Stennis a man, a public leader, or a respected citizen, he calls him "an individual of impeccable reputation." (Note that the Senator is not a group.) And consider the following quote:

> . . . *turn over the controversial tapes to an individual of his selection who was peculiarly qualified to perform this task, and to permit him to listen . . . as long as that individual felt it was necessary.*
>
> GEN. ALEXANDER M. HAIG, JR.

The tapes mustn't be turned over to a person, or to a man, or to a Congressman, or to a Senator, or even to a listener, but must be heard only by an *individual!*

Rivaling General Haig, Ron Ziegler manages to use "individual" twice in the same statement:

> *We do not have the responsibility for, and indeed will not provide, information on another individual's financial activities. I'm not charging any individual with maliciousness.*

Although Haig and Ziegler are both very good at the

12

impersonal, John Mitchell is the acknowledged master when it comes to using the word "individual." Mitchell even refuses to name Mr. Nixon, or call him "President," when speaking of him in the Senate hearings:

I think I know the individual. I know his reaction to things.

Although "individual" is the safest, easiest, and certainly the most common word used in DCD to achieve an impersonal tone, other words can also be used with striking effect for the purpose, such as "entity," another Washington favorite. At the 1972 Republican National Convention, Spiro Agnew defined his role as a "president's man," not a "competing entity." (He said later that he was not an "undetermined factor," which may be a mathematical reference, although mathematicians we have consulted are not at all sure.) And Robert Mardian is even more adept than Agnew with his "available to any entity." Evidently, whatever it is, is entities such as mobs, organizations, spies, governments, desks, buildings, lamps, kennels, turnips (?). And we mustn't slight Richard Helms's variation: ". . . usually he dealt with a defector."

The words "male" and "female" are also favorites with the impersonal set, as they are generic rather than specific. Notice the masterly way they can be used:

The cost of a grocery basket is felt by more families

than any other single item, particularly by those people who have to do the marketing, whether it's the male or the female of the family.

MELVIN LAIRD

But Anthony Ulasewicz manages to outdo the redoubtable Melvin Laird in this department with his striking statement, "I spoke to a male." It is possible that this sentence carries the impersonal to its ultimate.

As H. R. Haldeman said, "There was no discussion by name," a practice which Mr. Nixon exemplifies when he speaks of Clarence M. Kelley as a "name":

> ... *the way things broke, eventually we found another name with somewhat the same qualifications, although in this case not a judge—in this case a chief of police with former FBI experience.*

Sometimes it is necessary, however, to use names, so when you *must* use one, always use "Mr." before it, even if you are speaking of your closest friend. Never say "Bob told me John called," or "Alex asked Herbert to go." Instead, use as many "Mr.'s" as you can, as Ehrlichman does in this statement:

> *Mr. Magruder told me that Mr. Mitchell very vigorously criticized Mr. Liddy in Mr. Liddy's—to his face, so to speak, and that the second entry was not by reason*

14

of any prior planning on the part of either Mr. Mitchell or Mr. Magruder or others responsible, but was a reaction by Mr. Liddy to the heavy criticism that he received for the inadequate results of the first entry.

Or as John Mitchell does in this one:

Well, I am not sure that I can tell you very much about them other than the fact that somewhere along in the fall, Mr. Hunt had a telephone conversation with Mr. Colson, which, I think, and then later on, as I recall, covered the subject matter. Mr. Dean has got in the record a letter from Mr. Hunt to Mr. Colson, which I think is quite suggestive of the fact that he was being abandoned.

It is also possible to make something impersonal by combining a name with an impersonal designation, as Bernard Barker does in "We were assisting Mr. Hunt, who was a known factor in the time of the liberation of Cuba." (Perhaps it is a sign of status to be a "known factor" rather than an "undetermined factor.")

If worst comes to worst, however, and you can't think of *any* impersonals, you can always use *numbers.*

The fact that I had been directed to undertake these actions by the No. 2 and No. 3 men on the White House staff made it absolutely incomprehensible to me

that my actions in this regard could have been regarded
in any way as improper or unethical.

KALMBACH

So, you see, there is at your disposal a wealth of ways to sound impersonal. Study these examples carefully, practice them diligently, and soon you will be able to refer to your neighbors as "the male and the female in the neighboring domicile."

Lesson 2:

Be Obscure

I would feel that most of the conversations that took place in those areas of the White House that did have the recording system would in almost their entirety be in existence but the special prosecutor, the court, and, I think, the American people are sufficiently familiar with the recording system to know where the recording devices existed and to know the situation in terms of the recording process but I feel, although the process has not been undertaken yet in preparation of the material to abide by the court decision, really, what the answer to that question is.

RON ZIEGLER

Always speak in riddles. Obscurity is the stock-in-trade of the D.C. Dialect, since Washington officials must never say what they mean in language anyone can understand. Only peasants do that. Government spokesmen say very little in the most roundabout ways possible, and count as capital gain the resulting confusion. It profiteth officials little if their listeners understand them—for they are then

17

wide open for accusation and judgment. Therefore, they load their speech with words and phrases that are obscure, useless, and vague. Go and do likewise, and you will soon reap the rewards you so richly deserve.

Study the following example of obscurity, a perfect illustration of this lesson.

> *I do know that there was in the White House a desire to air this whole thing once the facts were known and it was hoped that a committee of the Congress would pick it up and would call witnesses and would expose how such a thing could happen in our governmental system today where the treachery was within the Government, if it was, or the treachery was in the think-tank apparatus if there was, and I am not suggesting there was, but whether there was, and who the individuals involved were, what their motivations were, and why this thing happened.*
>
> JOHN EHRLICHMAN

But circumlocution, a hallmark of Ehrlichman's speech, is not really necessary; you can achieve obscurity with short sentences as well. A minor politician, speaking of campaign spending, was recently heard to say that "federal funding must occur." You see—optimism and obscurity combined! If "funding" can "occur," it can "occur" anywhere. So money can sprout on trees, fall from heaven like manna, or breed in your slippers overnight. (The gentleman should be given credit for throwing in that nice bit of alliteration in "federal funding," too.)

The imprecise use of words offers an easy road to obscurity. Study, for instance, this sentence by Gen. Creighton Abrams: "I worry about any perceptions people hold generally, because historically they have often turned out to be wrong." The perceptions have turned out to be wrong? The people have turned out to be wrong? Does "any perceptions" mean *all* perceptions ever held? Perhaps if the "perceptions" had been held less "generally" they would have turned out to be right. You see how the talented General manages total and varied obscurity with an ostensibly simple statement.

Spiro Agnew has a tricky (and singular) way to create obscurity—a way you may also find enlightening. He does it by using unexplained figures of speech which haven't the remotest connection with expected imagery:

> *I think that this, left in an unresolved posture, could hurt the Republican Party.*

> *I think he* [the Vice President] *has a built-in disadvantage in having to be considered as a potential candidate, being in an office where what he's doing is constantly weighted against a candidate posture.*

You must admit that an "unresolved posture" is intriguing in itself, even if baffling. Perhaps someone is trying to pose

19

for a camera and is unable to get into the right posture, or some "thing" is forever being molded into an unattainable shape. "Candidate posture" may refer to politicians posing for television cameras, but the interpretation is difficult to uphold in the light of the fact that what someone is doing is being "weighted" against the posing. Another choice example of Agnew Obscurity occurs in the same interview, when Mr. Agnew says that "His philosophy and mine are very much on all fours with one another." What a brilliantly different metaphor—Philosophy as a beast. One can just see Deism as a baboon and Existentialism as a bull—their feet firmly planted and their "postures" set against each other. This sort of obscurity is only for the experts, however; as a novice you mustn't expect to come up with anything like it without years of practice.

Here is a technique easily acquired by the beginner, which will allow you to be vague and confound your friends and enemies alike: simply use the word "matter" as often as possible. "Matter" is very useful because it can refer to anything, everything, or nothing.

> *I also directed this group to prepare an accurate history of certain crucial national security matters which occurred under prior administrations, on which the government's records were incomplete.*
>
> RICHARD NIXON

20

There is a matter of judgment you make in connection with these areas.

JOHN MITCHELL

Barker's comment that "Compartmentation means you do not speak of these matters. You work on a need-to-know basis" is a masterpiece of murkiness, using the word "matter." But John Dean takes the cake when it comes to using the word, because his "matter" is going to "unravel."

I also told him that there was a long way to go before this matter would end, and that I certainly could make no assurance that the day would not come when this matter would start to unravel.

There are any number of phrases that will help you be obscure, and throwing such phrases around will help people identify you immediately as a DCD expert. Use phrases like the following (and don't worry about making sense):

a table-of-organization standpoint

for purposes to assist

the magnitude or co-magnitude of

21

operational function

certain transitionary periods

exerting an increased fiscal discipline

not in contemplation

Or make up your own obscure phrases, if you wish. Just be sure no one understands what you mean by them.

Here are some study guides that will help you master obscurity:

> *I don't recall the state of knowledge about the whole circuit of activities.*
>
> H. R. HALDEMAN

> *I told Liddy to transfer whatever capability he had from Muskie to McGovern.*
>
> STRACHAN

> *Our basic reference for managing the federal budget is the concept of the full-employment budget, that is, the relationship between receipts at full employment and outlays at full employment.*
>
> *But we are on the track we committed ourselves to be on . . .*
>
> ROY L. ASH

... doesn't care about the power of being close to the President; he wants the form of Oval Office entree, not the substance.

"a presidential aide"

Such a letter in the current atmosphere of Washington would become known and could be frankly electorally mortal.

LT. GEN. VERNON WALTERS

I am sure you are well aware that the President was not knowledgeable of the or involved in that and this would have been a derivative rub-off on many of something that was, would have been absolutely unfair and unjustified.

MITCHELL

It is only fitting that we end this lesson with, again, some examples of obscurity from General Haig, a past master of the subject. General Haig is so good at obscurity that it is difficult to pick examples from his words—it is rather like choosing from an embarrassment of riches. Sometimes the General manages a little gem like ". . . we requested that both Senators proceed from out of town Friday afternoon," but most of his efforts are much longer and more complicated, like this one:

Had he chosen that option, he could have resigned,

23

with all of the implications that that would have had for the participants and for the American people to digest and make their own judgment with respect to the validity of that course of action and the course of action pursued by the President. An option of that is: he could have delayed; he could have waited, and perhaps waited until further justification developed for a resumption of his needs, should they have developed.

If William Faulkner were alive today, he would surely be green with envy of such complex sentence structure! Yet even better in some ways is this last example by General Haig, although not as long or complex. Study it carefully, and know that when you can create obscurity like this, you have arrived:

I want to say this very carefully and very precisely, but certainly, certainly any foreign leader, whether he be friend or potential foe, must in a period of turmoil here at home make his calculations without the unity, the permanency, the strength and resilience of this government in a way that had to take consideration of this tape issue into mind.

Lesson 3:

Be Pompous

... availed themselves of access to the President's evening reading via the typewritten page.

JOHN EHRLICHMAN

Never hesitate to sound pompous by using inflated language. By the skillful use of bombast, Washington officials advertise their status as VIPs. Lofty ideas must be couched in lofty language; therefore, down-to-earth, mundane, specific words and phrases are scorned by People in Authority. Therefore, load your speech with long, Latinate terms, and soon you will receive the respect you deserve!

In DCD, no one "does his job"; one tries to "perform as many of these functions as possible." Daniel Ellsberg didn't "hand out" or "release" documents; he "disseminated" them. It is never "the case"; it is "the case in this area." One never says "I had," but "I had come into possession of"; never "I knew," but "it was my understanding"; never "got complicated," but "a great many systems evolved"; never "according to the evidence," but "according to documentary evidence at hand."

The list of pompous words is endless. One of the most striking is the term "confidentiality," as in the following:

> *... with the least intrusion of presidential con-*
> *fidentiality ...*
>
> CHARLES A. WRIGHT

> *... the confidentiality of the office of President ...*

> *... the confidentiality of conversations between ...*

> *Further, it would create a precedent that Presidents are*
> *required to submit to judicial demands that purport to*
> *override presidential determinations on requirements*
> *for confidentiality.*
>
> NIXON

Mr. Nixon leans heavily on this word, but we advise you not to get carried away with the suffix "ity"—otherwise you might find yourself turning words like "official" into "officiality," "financial" into "financiality," "presidential" into "presidentiality," "judicial" into "judiciality," "evidential" into "evidentiality," "crucial" into "cruciality," etc. So go slowly at first. Even though such constructions are well taken in the dialect, you should take it an "ity" bit at a time.

If you're a lawyer, you probably won't have any trouble thinking of pompous words and phrases—which is one good reason to become a lawyer in the first place. Look at these "lawyer-isms":

> *I can't recall all the exculpatory things I tried to do.*
> *... to maintain the fiduciary obligation not to disclose that which was confided in me.*
> > MARDIAN

> *... an accusatory forum.*

> *... investigatory organization.*
> > EHRLICHMAN

But you don't have to become a lawyer in order to sound pompous; almost anyone can learn. Just remember to substitute Latinate words for native Anglo-Saxon words—that is, never use a little word when you can use a big word. For instance, never say "carry out," say "effectuate":

> *The purpose of the group is to effectuate community-wide coordination and secure the benefits of community-wide analysis and estimating.*
> > top secret memo by Nixon aides

Never say "certain," say "specified":

> These in turn had included authorization for surreptitious entry—breaking and entering, in effect—on specified categories of targets in specified situations related to national security.
>
> NIXON *

Never say "begin," say "commence":

> . . . it was not until several weeks ago, . . . that a review of the tapes by him was commenced.
>
> J. FRED BUZHARDT

Never say "tell" or "talk," say "relay" or "conversation":

> Dean has testified we left the meeting together and he had a conversation with me at which he cautioned me against relaying this fund-raising request to Mitchell.
>
> RICHARD MOORE

Never say "caused by," say "attributable to":

> The major breakthrough . . . was directly attributable to the continuing efforts . . .
>
> ANON.

---

* Mr. Nixon's understandable concern for national security has earned him the enviable nickname of Lord of the Spies.

It is forbidden in DCD to say "I remember," because that would be much too simple and direct. Instead, you must say "to the best of my recollection," or "according to my recollection," or "as I recall." Try something like this by John Mitchell's lawyer:

> *Our best recollection is that it never came to our attention until it was in the form in which it eventuated, which was the civil action that was brought.*
>
> WILLIAM G. HUNDLEY

This statement is especially fine, as it uses the bloated word "eventuated," and creates total obscurity as well as pomposity through awkward sentence structure!

It is also forbidden in the dialect to use the words "then" or "now." Here is a selection of pompous quotes to use in place of them.

> *There was just no alternative at that point in time.*
>
> JOHN W. DEAN, III

> *At one point in time he indicated to me that I was not to disburse any money without Mr. Mitchell's approval.*
>
> HUGH W. SLOAN, JR.

> *I can tell you that whatever point in time that was that it was my opinion that the CIA was involved . . .*
>
> MARDIAN

29

At a point in time in connection with the Pentagon Papers theft, a whole series of events took place.

EHRLICHMAN

Dean at this time point was clearly in charge of any matters relating to Watergate.

HALDEMAN

I do recall him being in Washington a couple of times in this time frame.

FREDERICK LARUE

The word "when" should be used sparingly, and only when you can't think of an alternative. Instead of beginning questions with "when," try Senator Weicker's method: "At what point in time did you . . . ?" When you achieve finesse, you can come up with statements like this, which combine pomposity with redundancy:

I am trying as best I can to recall what impressions I had at this particular point in time.

CAULFIELD

The word "before" does not exist in DCD, and "previous" is seldom used. It is considered chic to say "prior to" and "prior" instead, and there are innumerable ways to use these favorites.

a prior episode

I had no prior knowledge of

in my prior office

prior to the meeting

under prior administrations

prior to the beginning of

Do not forget and use the old English word "before."

Lt. Gen. Vernon Walters is an expert at pomposity and you can learn much by studying his words. These remarkable examples were delivered in the course of one afternoon's testimony at the Senate hearings!

He was exploring this option . . .

. . . a recapitulation of various pieces of information.

I transmitted the message to Mr. Gray.

I must associate myself with Mr. Helms's answer.

There was a differentiation in what the three men asked me to do.

That would have been circumventing my channels.

Of course you can't expect to become an expert at pomposity overnight, but you can study and practice and develop your ability. And remember, what you are going for are the really flashy combinations—those phrases and sentences which combine obscurity with pomposity. The following, for example, contain just the right touch of class.

I think you reach a point of reasonability . . .

WILLIAM E. CASSELMAN

. . . a hard evidentiary conclusion.

EHRLICHMAN

. . . it costs $7 to $8 per hour for plumbers and electricians when installation forces are utilized to perform such tasks.

MAJ. GEN. VERNE L. BOWERS

We are shopping elsewhere to fill out the normal replenishment.

GERALD WARREN

The principle vehicle in this respect was a daily staff meeting.

MAURICE STANS

I objected to seeing Mr. McCord, but finally Mr. Dean got my concurrence to do so.

CAULFIELD

But Mr. Kalmbach had no involvement in the form or nature of that contribution.

JAMES H. O'CONNOR

. . . and ask wherein you differentiate . . .

SEN. HERMAN TALMADGE

I was not able to get across to you the genesis of my thinking.

ATTORNEY JOHN J. WILSON

. . . in this frame of reference . . .

all DCD speakers

If your efforts at pomposity sound sanctimonious, don't worry about it—almost all public statements in DCD have a ring of sanctimony. Note, for example, the great piety of these statements:

His message was the voice of reason which went a long way toward putting the whole situation in better perspective.

GOV. RONALD REAGAN on Nixon's speech of August 15, 1973

33

I am sure that if he had looked into my eyes and I had looked into his eyes and we had invoked the names of our wives, I am sure I would remember that solemn occasion . . .

EHRLICHMAN

God bless America, and God bless each and every one of you.

NIXON,

Sentiments such as these are really indispensable in maintaining your image as a public leader of upright character and untarnished morals, so feel free to be publicly pious.

We end this lesson with two superb examples of pomposity—examples which will give you something to emulate. The first not only uses that fine word "implement," but contains a misplaced adverb as well!

I want to emphasize that if you implement your plans as we discussed, the President will adequately recognize you.

WILLIAM MARUMOTO, White House memo

It is hard not to conjure up a picture of a president bowing ceremoniously in the Japanese manner. But good as this quote is, the next really outdoes it, as it is not only a masterpiece of pomposity, but even contains a sentence fragment.

> *It will give us a massive capability of pulling together evidentiary material, pulling it together as only a computer can do. In a reasonably instantaneous time frame.*
>
> JOSEPH PECORE

The fact that DCD speakers are eternally pompous explains the otherwise curious lack of interjections in the dialect, at least in public. After all, interjections indicate enthusiasm and emotion—qualities which deflate pomposity. Think about it. If DCD people said things like "My God!" or "Alas!" or "Up yours!" they would lose their cool. And in DCD you must keep your cool at all times. So be sure to rid your public speech of things like "Hell fire!" and "No shit!?!" and "Mercy me!"

Lesson 4:

Be Evasive

It's not a question of trying to set up a system that would falsify records; it was a question of setting up a special reporting procedure.

JERRY W. FRIEDHEIM

Now that you've learned to be impersonal, obscure, and pompous, you must learn to be evasive and euphemistic—that is, never call a spade a spade. Call it a "long-handled implement," or a "designated gardening instrument," but never call it a spade. If you refer to your wife as a wife, to your dog as a dog, to your friends as friends, to criminals as criminals, to burglary as burglary, to spying as spying, you've got a lot to learn. In DCD, burglars are called "operatives," lies are called "inoperatives," criminals are called "intelligence agents," and spies are called "plumbers." Take the subject of lying, for example. Here are some ways to talk about lies in DCD:

After a very careful review, I have determined that this statement of mine is not precisely accurate.

NIXON

McCord's statement does not fully reflect my best recollections.

CAULFIELD

I think I can put it on the basis that I had a pretty strong feeling that his testimony was not going to be entirely accurate.

MITCHELL

Questioner: *Do you think Mr. Hoover lied?*
Ehrlichman: *No, I think he papered the file.*

You'll note that Ehrlichman combines euphemism with total obscurity, which is quite a talent. The question is left unanswered, and the questioner is left with a mental picture of Mr. Hoover gluing wallpaper to a filing cabinet.

Never say you "knew" or "learned" when you can use a nice, amorphous-sounding term like "became aware." DCD experts ooze amorphisms.

I became aware [of payments to the Watergate conspirators] in the fall sometime.

37

I became aware or had a belief that it was a false story.
MITCHELL

I was aware that such a [special investigations] *unit was set up.*

The President had no awareness of such acts.
HALDEMAN

I was aware there was a need for a defense fund.
EHRLICHMAN

Never be so blunt as to answer questions with the simple, damning words "yes" or "no." Listen to the experts:

I'm not your best witness on that.
EHRLICHMAN

I would rather be excused from drawing my own conclusion on that at this point in time.
DEAN

I made no moral judgment on it at all.

I was not called upon to condone or condemn.

38

I am not sure yet where that failure was ... because only then will it be determined where the failure wasn't.

HALDEMAN

It is my opinion, Senator, that particularly during the month of April and the succeeding intervening period of time, he has done exactly what he should have done in lowering the boom.

MITCHELL

Mitchell not only avoids a simple yes or no, but introduces the cliché, "lowering the boom," which, cleverly enough, turns out to mean nothing at all. And if someone accuses you of destroying vital documents, baffle them with a linguistic jewel like this:

Shredding is an activity that has been foreign to my nature.

EHRLICHMAN

One of the most effective methods of sidestepping answers is the use of the "unexpected." Notice how Haldeman evokes thoughts of The Great Pumpkin, thereby disrupting the train of thought:

There is no initiative and there's no stuff beyond the vegetable.

Dean and Ehrlichman are also adept at surprising their questioners:

Let me give you my overall first.

DEAN

He doesn't think they'll give him a chance to come back unless he comes running at them and strokes them.

Search may be a term of art.

Carte blanche means something less than an absolute run of the place.

EHRLICHMAN

Military spokesmen help out with some good euphemisms about bombing, like "strikes," and "protective reaction strikes," and "efforts to achieve a cease-fire." This last phrase is especially useful, as it can cover a multitude of sins, or, in this case, a multitude of bombings.

Gen. Earle G. Wheeler outdoes them all with a euphemism that can only be classed as a deny-everything-including-logic type. Speaking of the Pentagon giving erroneous information to the Congress, the General blandly says that there was "no intent to deceive."

Of course Jerry Friedheim, Pentagon spokesman (and DCD expert), is no slouch when it comes to euphemism, and occasionally he outdoes even the generals. When confronted with the *New York Times* eyewitness account of the damage inflicted on Hanoi's Bach Mai hospital by American bombing, Friedheim dismissed the report as "enemy propaganda." Later, when millions of Americans had seen films of the hospital's devastation on television, Friedheim conceded that "some limited accidental damage" had been done. Delighted with its euphemistic and evasive spokesman, the Defense Department awarded Mr. Friedheim its Medal for Distinguished Public Service, which came with this citation: "He has provided with faultless professionalism clear, concise, accurate and timely information concerning the worldwide activities of the Department of Defense." Such an honor should dispel any doubt about the efficacy of the dialect.

(Be careful that you do not slip and admit a best-evaded truth, as Melvin Laird does in a Pentagon memo to General Wheeler on how to keep the bombing of Cambodia from nosy reporters. He suggests that B-52s hit Cambodia along with the B-52s attacking assigned targets in South Vietnam and Laos. "Strikes on these latter targets will provide a resemblance to normal operations, thereby providing a credible story for replies to press inquiries." If Mr. Laird had stuck conscientiously to DCD, even in his private memos, this bit of truth would never have seen the light of day.)

Ron Ziegler must be given a lot of credit for his effort to outdo the Pentagon in evasive and euphemistic statements, although civilian sincerity is rarely a match for military professionalism. But there are times when Mr. Ziegler seems positively inspired. When asked by reporters whether allied troops were getting ready to invade Laos, he responded with the following verbal gyration:

The President is aware of what is going on in Southeast Asia. That is not to say that anything is going on in Southeast Asia.

And DCD is eternally enriched by a Ziegler statement that puts him right up there with the Pentagon top brass. The press secretary said the purpose of the resumption of the bombing of Hanoi during Christmas 1972 was to instill in Hanoi peace negotiators "a spirit of good will and a constructive attitude." What class!

There is really no end of ways to be evasive in the D.C. Dialect. The following quotes show how easy it is to avoid incriminating yourself and yet manage to accuse others without using names:

[the offer was] *from the very highest levels of the White House.*

CAULFIELD

Given normal reporting channels I worked through, it

was my assumption without question that it was going to the President.

DEAN

In retrospect, it appears that restraint should have been somewhat greater.

ARTHUR BURNS

The number of euphemisms in the dialect is boundless. This statement, for instance, talks about spying without once mentioning the word:

On June 25, the committee submitted a report which included specific options for expanded intelligence operations, and on July 23 the agencies were notified by memorandum of the options approved.

NIXON,

It is also possible to talk about breaking and entering without using the words:

. . . to cause an entry under illegal circumstances.

WILSON

In fact, it's possible to talk about almost anything euphemistically. Here are some hints: Never say "He was about to lose his job," when you can say that his "employment status was very murky at that time." Don't say

43

"He was a liar," when you can say "He was less than honest." And never say—simply—"I've been used," when you can say

> *Yes, if they had knowledge of what has been alleged to be the true purpose of this and did not inform me, I have been used.*

KALMBACH

But whatever you say, don't make the mistake of exposing the use of language for evasion, as a military spokesman does in this far too revealing quote:

> *Obviously, the Army will not, as far as we can see, be called upon to fight in a "national war of liberation." Another term will be found to describe it.*

When you have exhausted all other techniques of evasive language and are pinned to the wall with a direct question you don't want to answer, just throw logic and common sense to the wind and come out with something like this:

> *Whether the term used was "mortally wounded" or not, I do not know. Some believe that it was, some believe that it wasn't. That's irrelevant. He could have said that.*

NIXON

44

Lesson 5:

Be Repetitious

Mitchell did some markup on some of it—I cannot recall what he marked on these papers—indicating his approval, did not indicate it in any formal sense by initiating it or writing, just indicated the project was approved.

JEB STUART MAGRUDER

Lesson 5 is a snap; all you have to do is repeat yourself, over and over and over and over. When you find a word that sounds good, use it two or three times in the same sentence. Or say the same thing several different ways. And add as many unnecessary words as possible. What you're aiming for is total boredom, which will prevent listeners from following your train of thought. And keep in mind that you do *not* want to make your meaning *clear*. Unaffected speech and lucidity have *no* place in DCD.

Consider the simple word "situation." Accomplished DCD speakers rely heavily on this word to produce total saturation in listeners. After hearing the word several hundred times, listeners tend to enter a state of inattention akin to hypnosis, in which they are unable to judge the value of what they hear. Use the word continually in phrases such as the following:

in the foregoing situation

in an emergency situation

in a crisis situation

this fact situation

a national security situation

As you can see, each of these nouns could have been used alone without the redundant "situation," but if each had been, the sentence would have been shorter and clearer. Mr. Nixon is particularly good at this sort of thing. In one press conference he talks of a "complex situation set-up," a really choice example of redundancy!

Certain words and phrases—like "conditions," "circumstances," "state," "state of affairs"—are simply not acceptable in DCD if "situation" can be used in their place. (It is permissible to use "circumstances" occasionally, particularly if you can work it into the same sentence with "situation," as Haldeman does in "It would depend on the circumstances—on the individual situation.") It is quite important to avoid these words, and use "situation," even if you have to rearrange a sentence to include that ubiquitous word. Rather than "The tapes were voice-actuating," say "It was a voice-actuating situation." Rather than "in this condition," say "in these types of situations." Rather than "in this regard," say "regarding this situation." Instead of "under those circumstances," say "in a situation like that." Instead of "under those conditions," say "in those specified situations." Or you can just sprinkle "situation" about indiscriminately as Haldeman does in these examples:

It depends on the circumstances and the situation . . .

. . . there has been embarrassment from the overall situation.

. . . and not the kind of situation where you could walk away on Monday.

. . . given the time situation . . .

. . . dealing with the situation, rather than dealing with the facts of the situation.

The word "facility" is almost as popular a redundancy as "situation," and is gaining ground every day. There is no longer such a thing as an airport; there is an "airport facility." No longer do old people go to nursing homes; they go to "nursing home facilities." No one builds a building; he builds a "facility." There are no more garbage dumps; there are only "disposal facilities." A new hospital is a new "medical care facility," a new school is a new "educational facility," a new radio station is a new "media facility," a new prison is a new "correctional facility," and so on. Who knows?—we may not be far from the day when churches and synagogues become "spiritual facilities."

Every DCD expert also has some pet redundancies. For example, John Mitchell prefers "subject matter,"

I am sure that that subject matter has crossed my mind . . .

The President called Mr. Ehrlichman on the subject matter while we were there.

So obviously, the subject matter of Watergate came up . . .

. . . to the particular time when there were two subject matters contained in that discussion there, one of which had to do, of course, with his termination and the other had to do with the other subject matter.

But he also likes "area."

I do think there were enough discussions in the area, in the general area, to the point where I think the general subject matter would have come out . . .

. . . you have two risks that have to be weighed and certainly it is the case in this area.

It depends entirely upon the area, Mr. Chairman.

I would have to qualify that with respect to certain areas that might involve national security . . .

. . . they were not about to go and incriminate themselves in those particular areas.

Hugh Sloan shows a bit more imagination than Mr. Mitchell in his choice of redundant words:

I essentially asked for guidance.

I went to this cocktail party on the boat.
I guess my mood would be essentially anger.

They were essentially in a debriefing process of people who had been before the grand jury.

A favorite redundancy of many master speakers of the dialect is "focus."

I don't believe I focused on it at the time.
MITCHELL

I did not at the time focus on whether or not it was legal or illegal. I focused on the object—which was to examine the files without his consent.
DAVID R. YOUNG, JR.

GENERAL HAIG: *I didn't focus in on it in any way. It's not the kind of thing I'd focus on.*

RICHARD BEN-VENISTE: *When did you focus on it?*

GENERAL HAIG: *I think I focused on it the day Mr. Buzhardt came over here.*

And note this rhythmic redundancy from the Oval Office:

NIXON: *You sort of condemned him by—*

EHRLICHMAN: *Negative inference.*

NIXON: *Negative inference.*

HALDEMAN: *We're all condemned by negative inference.*

50

Almost any word or phrase can be used redundantly, of course. Learn from this fine example:

> *. . . which he feels is very vital to the national security of the country.*
>
> EHRLICHMAN

How something can be more vital than vital is a question that can probably be answered only by Madison Avenue.

The following phrases show how two words can be used in place of one for instant redundancy:

> *There were manifold and compound complexities . . .*

> *. . . individual members and groups of members . . .*

> *. . . raised a cautionary warning . . .*
>
> EHRLICHMAN

Surely, "cautionary warning" deserves some sort of award, like Redundancy of the Year, or something. However, a close runner-up might be the following from Mr. Nixon, who also shows a fine grasp of repetition, when he "begins" a "beginning."

> *By mid-1969, my administration had begun a number of highly sensitive foreign policy initiatives.*

Not to be outdone, Raymond C. Zumwalt comes up with this entry:

> *The family-locator system would turn on the pick-up device at his location, wherever he would be.*

It is good to know that his location is wherever he is. And Herbert L. Porter, no slouch in this sort of competition, comes in a strong contender with this effort:

> *I put the photographing of a document in the same category as Xeroxing a document . . . if you are taking a picture of it one way, you are taking a picture of it another way. So I did not think it was illegal. I thought it was very surreptitious, but I did not think it was illegal.*

There are also ways in the D.C. Dialect to talk about time without mentioning the word—all of which are delightfully redundant. Study these illustrations from Haldeman:

> *Following this sequence of events . . .*

> *I came back to Washington for a several day period.*

> *. . . on a frequency of about once a week.*

52

Of course, phrases like these are not easy to come up with; the average speaker of English just doesn't think of things like "several day period."

For beginners, it's best to stick to straight repetition as these speakers do:

It was a snafu and a mistake to send the Congressional report . . .

LAIRD

My own personal view is . . .

. . . in the world abroad.

SEN. EDWARD J. GURNEY

. . . let me, let me correct you, sir . . . in terms of those times, of those times . . . with his record, with his record . . . and that's my view . . . But my view . . . more than I want, more than my family wants.

NIXON

. . . carry out both of these two objectives.

HALDEMAN

We feel duty bound to warn you that you run the risk of saying things that are inadvertently funny in your pursuit of redundancy. A state party chairman, visiting in

Washington, was heard to say that "Committee members are elected people," as if there were any danger that committee members would be elected animals.

If you practice very hard, it is very likely that at the near point in a given sequence of time you'll be very, very good at repeating yourself over and over when you engage in a conversational situation or write a memo to any individual or group of individuals.

Lesson 6:

Be Awkward

My own personal view is that I think these hearings are damaging this government seriously, the nation, and also its relation in the world abroad.

SEN. EDWARD GURNEY

Make your speech as clumsy as possible. Of course the awkward path of DCD rhetoric is tortuous indeed for the beginner: the sentence structure twists and turns unexpectedly; made-up words cross paths with shifted parts of speech; points of view shift back and forth like sand; the passive voice is the soil for the clumsiest of constructions; and wordiness virtually obscures meaning. But take heart. You can conquer this rhetorical wasteland if you are strong-stomached and have learned all the previous lessons. After all, if you know how to be pompous, obscure, repetitious, impersonal, and evasive, your rhetoric is already awkward.

The following examples will simply point the way to *professional* clumsiness. In addition, they will help you through those daily language crises when your soul cries out to speak English. When these times come upon you, think of the rewards that await your mastering of DCD, and you will find renewed strength to speak as awkwardly as possible.

The following samples illustrate the professional touch given to potentially simple sentences by DCD speakers. You'll note that simplicity is out and "compound-convoluted-complex" is in.

Mr. Dash, I think you and I have gone over to the point where we have established that the White House horror stories have come out in connection with the problem at that particular time. And there wasn't a question of lifting the tent slightly in order to get—with respect to one individual or another. It was a "keep the lid on," and no information volunteered.

MITCHELL

My actions in the period immediately following the break-in which involved the raising of funds to provide for the legal defense of the Watergate defendants and for the support of their families were prompted in the belief that it was proper and necessary to discharge what I assumed to be a moral obligation that has arisen in some manner unknown to me by reasons of earlier events.

KALMBACH

56

I know that it has been testified that such a request was made and was not carried out and I am not familiar with the specifics of the reason for the request, but there were times when there was a very definite interest in the activities of Senator Kennedy, some political and some not political at all, but in relation to trips that he made with regard to early release of P.O.W.'s and matters dealing with the North Vietnamese and the peace settlement efforts that were underway.

HALDEMAN

These next sentences achieve awkwardness by mangling what should be parallel sentence structure—an achievement no amateur can hope to copy:

In addition to the steps already taken, we will take whatever actions are necessary—including gasoline consumption must be decreased.

WILLIAM E. SIMON

I have been under the impression that your committee was going to investigate paper shredding and possibly other activities hiding public business from the public rather than to obtain a shredder and shredding on its own.

REP. WAYNE L. HAYS

If you can't think fast enough to create whole sentences

that are awkward, you might try interchanging parts of speech—a practice called "functional shift" by linguists, and much prized by DCD speakers. Functional shift is basic to the English language and serves to enrich it, but recently we have heard some elitist language snobs complain that such shifts in DCD are unnecessary. These "experts" claim that DCD speakers create elephantine words to supplant perfectly good words already in the language, and needless, ugly nouns out of verbs, verbs out of nouns, nouns out of adjectives, and adjectives out of nouns. One snob actually referred to this creative practice in DCD as "functional shit." Such vulgar complaints are best answered with silence!

Take a noun phrase like "national security," for instance; instead of using it as a noun, try using it as an adjective.

national security area

national security activities

national security operations
                    NIXON

national security readiness
                    JAMES SCHLESINGER

national security characteristic

58

national security overtones

national security implications

GEN. ROBERT E. CUSHMAN

As you can see, once you hit upon a happy phrase with an important-sounding ring to it, you can use it over and over, thereby adding repetition to your speech. And repetition gives an extra bonus—soon the phrase means nothing at all! With practice, you can come full circle—through functional shift to pomposity to repetition to total obscurity.

The most common functional shift in the dialect is from noun to adjective, a device which General Haig illustrates here by using the noun "profile" as an awkward and confusing adjective:

> ... *what had become a highly profiled and extremely controversial issue* ...

Here are some more examples of this device; see if you can guess who said them.

not an operation division

our two constituent clients were

issue stances

had a very strong friendship urge

from a hindsight standpoint

You may have recognized these last two examples as Ehrlichman's, because they're so robust and vigorous. Ehrlichman's functional shift must be the envy of every dialect speaker in Washington!

The rarest types of functional shift in the dialect are adjective-to-verb and verb-to-noun. A noted public figure provides a charming example of the former in this comment:

> *Congress has got to determine whether the things you've been talking about unfit him.*
>
> NELSON ROCKEFELLER

And Mr. Schlesinger gives a rare illustration of the shift from verb to noun in this:

> *There is the additional likelihood that if the training standdown lasts long enough, accident rates may increase.*

And you thought "Stand down!" was an imperative verb form favored by the military!

The most noticeable way to speak awkwardly is to make up words. Invented words are called neologisms by linguists, and most of them ring with pedantry and obscurity, and stand out from normal words. Novices had best approach them with caution. Study these two examples by Herbert Stein and you'll see how tricky it is to distort ordinary English words:

. . . people who have a necessitous demand for . . .

. . . to get us over certain transitionary periods to a situation in which we will have reasonable price stability . . .

As you can see, Stein has translated the English words "necessary" and "transitional" into DCD, which takes a bit of doing, no question about it. We stand amazed at a mentality that can create a word like "necessitous," but perhaps we shouldn't be surprised, as D.C. Dialect speakers constantly come up with neologisms like the following: "disaggregation," "deracialization," "survivability," "prenotify." It's really rather hard to think up English words that are as strong as "deracialization," or "disaggregation," or "survivability." As for "prenotify," it must mean to notify before you notify(!)(?).

Haldeman, as always, is right up there with the best with ". . . for *trashing* and other sorts of activities." It is possible that "trashing" has to do with handling garbage as a career, but Haldeman's natural propensity for obscurity will doubtless prevent our ever knowing. His "It was not discussed in terms of scapegoatism . . ." is also passing strange.

Occasionally a speaker comes up with a neologism that can only be called eccentric. Melvin Laird manages to do this when he makes a normally intransitive verb transitive in this sentence:

I didn't falsify any question—I no-commented *it.*

And Senator Howard Baker's "communicatory" is almost as odd:

. . . those are valid communicatory *forms.*

But those of you who are sensitive to verb usage may balk at this one:

We have no intention of freeing up *the price of gasoline.*

SIMON

One of the reasons that practitioners of the dialect like neologisms is that made-up words are substitutes for traditional words—and ordinary mortals use traditional words. Tack on a prefix or a suffix—or both—as the mood strikes you, and *voila!*

. . . if you start depoliticizing things, you better watch out or you depoliticize yourself.

WILLIAM SAXBE

Some critics of the dialect have expressed dislike for this particular neologism, pointing out that the word suggests a delousing process, or being dunked in sheep dip. In our opinion, the critics are simply envious of the imagination shown by DCD speakers.

One warning, however, about making up words. "Neologism" is also a term used by psychiatrists to denote words invented by psychotics, so be careful of using phrases like the following:

stroking call

trigger a clue

talking papers

leak problem

defamatory leaks

Lord High Executioner for Leaks

You see the danger. Instead of sounding like a Washington official, you might end up sounding like a Washington nut.

When you weary of making up new words and shifting old ones about, you might like to play with point of view. It's really quite easy. If you begin in first person, switch to second person right in the middle of a sentence or paragraph. Or switch from second to third person, or whatever you fancy. It's an artful way to make your speech awkward and confuse your listeners at the same time. Here's a good way to do it:

A U.S. Attorney's letter is not the kind of thing that makes you comfortable.

AGNEW

The talented Melvin Laird goes one better in the next statement; he manages to use all three points of view in three short sentences—a talent possibly acquired during his years as Secretary of Defense.

Sometimes people are caught up in a series of circumstances where you have to make certain changes. And I think those changes will be made. I don't think you have to have a big announcement over something like that.

In this next example, George Shultz, speaking in his former role as Secretary of the Treasury, conveniently takes himself out of the group that must "tighten up," leaving everyone guessing who has to do it.

We have to get back down to that 4 per cent rate and you get there by tightening up.

When you tire of changing point of view in mid-stream, you can always try using verbs in the passive—rather than the active—voice, a practice which almost automatically guarantees awkward sentence structure. The use of the passive also leave the impression that you have not "done," but have "been done unto," an impression that will serve you well if anyone has the temerity to question any of your Important Activities.

The passive also has the effect of disguising the agent.

I was *so* advised.

Information was imparted *to me* . . .

. . . was *never* disclosed *to me*.

MARDIAN

I was motivated *solely by my concern for the presidential campaign in which we* were engaging.

LARUE

It is possible to combine passive voice, awkward construction, and total lack of logic—although it is not an easy thing to do. This statement is possibly unprecedented, even in the amazing world of DCD:

And passage of time alone is never . . . used to move a man from one list to the other.

LT. GEN. DANIEL JAMES, JR.

65

As a finale to this lesson, we'd like to present a classic of awkwardness—a sentence that probably helped earn its creator the nickname "Generally Vague."

I don't have to describe for you some of the backdrop of this morning's atmosphere, but, that being true and having experienced an additional week of some fairly high tensions in our international business, the President concluded, after very painful and anguishing discussion with me, with his counsel, that the circumstances were sufficiently grave in the context of our national attitudes on this issue—which I must say in my view have been subject to a great deal of misunderstanding, a great deal of misinformation over the past weekend—but, in the light of this situation, the President decided that he would abandon on this occasion these very strongly held and long-held convictions that he, as President of these United States, has the obligation, indeed, to protect the rights and prerogatives of this office, not only for himself but for subsequent Presidents in our upcoming history.

GENERAL HAIG

Nadel

Lesson 7:

Be Incorrect

Yes, I guess the Kennedy crowd is just laying in the bushes waiting to make their move.

RICHARD M. NIXON

Always try to speak wrong. One of the main character-istics of the D.C. Dialect is incorrectness, so you must cultivate faulty diction, confusing syntax, misused reflex-ives, vague pronoun references, and, for special occa-sions, incomplete sentences. Speakers of the dialect must, after all, spice their speech with their own special season-ing of misused words and grammatical errors. If they did not, someone might suspect them of being interested in the English language.

In order to render DCD palatable, you must begin with small portions of debasement. Start with some erroneous or misused words like the following:

Segretti should continue out in the field, functioning somewhat independent.

STRACHAN

67

I would have went *back to its original state. The person changing the tape would probably not have realized that it had* went *through its switching phase* . . .

RAYMOND C. ZUMWALT

. . . *indicated to me that he had not learned of it* . . . *except* just soon.

RICHARD KLEINDIENST

You will find illiteracies useful if only for the reaction you get. Listeners are momentarily stunned, which renders them incapable of figuring out what you have just said. Try something like this:

. . . *rather than* separate *them* out *from Watergate* . . .

NIXON

Ehrlichman, obviously emulating his boss, also uses "separate out," thereby identifying himself with the chief spokesman of the dialect. Not to be outdone, Mardian manages to say "involved back," but it's hard to get the best of the top spokesmen when they come up with gems like these:

I didn't respond clear enough.

EHRLICHMAN

Subsequently to that . . .

HALDEMAN

68

These two further show their skill by mispronouncing words—a surefire means of drawing attention to the words and away from the meaning. Ehrlichman's "defen*dants*," and "individual *'coop',*" are certainly as good as Haldeman's "irrevōcably."

Misused prepositional phrases can provide some rewarding incorrectness—

. . . between our team . . .

. . . amongst each other . . .
                              BERNARD L. BARKER

When the matter was closed out as between you and Mr. Sullivan . . .
                              EHRLICHMAN

. . . and see where the conflict is between you and he.
                              SENATOR TALMADGE

but misleading prepositional phrases also pay dividends in confusion:

It was not in contemplation.
                              EHRLICHMAN

. . . to improve coordination among the intelligence community . . .
                              NIXON

This next prepositional phrase gives us some insight into the slowdown of "great causes" after the election; Mr. Nixon seems to be saying that he was elected to carry these causes forward only in November of 1972!

There are these and other great causes that we were elected overwhelmingly to carry forward in November of 1972.

Critics of the dialect often say that DCD speakers add unnecessary reflexive pronouns all the time because they don't know the difference between the nominative and the objective cases and think the reflexive sounds somehow more grammatical. Nothing could be further from the truth; DCD speakers just *like* the reflexive because of the added "weight" it gives to a sentence, as in the following examples:

. . . to transmit . . . conversations out of the room itself.
MCCORD

. . . the domestic scene itself . . .
AGNEW

. . . not what the individuals who were participating in

that meeting, certainly Dean and myself, had in mind.
MITCHELL

So remember to use "myself" in place of "I" and "me" as often as possible.

The frequent absence of subject-verb agreement in the dialect is almost as effective as the strange prepositional phrases and all that "reflexing." These speakers, burdened as they are with Heavy Official Duties, haven't time to make distinctions between singular and plural subjects. Witness this, for example:

> The questions *of how many people to employ, the efforts to be expended in each state, the determination of the relative use of direct mail, personal solicitation and media advertising, the kinds of appeals to voters, and the entire gamut of the political effort* was developed.
>
> STANS

> ... neither *one of them* are *true* ...
>
> EHRLICHMAN

The singular–plural syndrome naturally spills over into pronoun usage, as you see here:

> Everybody *is attempting to do* their *thing and responding in a patriotic fashion.*
>
> SIMON

These next quotes illustrate not only incorrect pronoun

71

agreement, but show the strong quality of camaraderie among DCD speakers as well:

> *Dean's theory is that both Mitchell and Magruder both realize that they now have their ass in this thing, and that they are trying to untangle it.*
>
> HALDEMAN

> *Let's all go out and tromp their ass.*
>
> NIXON

References which are born of evasion and nourished in obscurity are the very heart of incorrectness, and as such, cannot be ignored by those seriously interested in mastering this dialect. The beauty of these vague antecedents is that not even a taped telephone conversation or recording can reveal who or what the "bugees" are talking about. Study these examples:

> *When* problems *arise which involve areas of interest to agencies or departments not members of the group,* they *shall be invited, at the discretion of the group to join the group as observers and participants in those discussions of interest to them.*
>
> top secret memo

You see what a clever tactic is being used here; language

72

like this in top secret memos or tapes prevents enemies or friends from understanding the contents!

> *The President then referred to the fact that Hunt had been promised executive clemency. He said that* he *had discussed* this matter *with Ehrlichman and, contrary to instructions that Ehrlichman had given Colson not to talk to the President about* it, *that Colson had also discussed* it *with* him *later.* He *expressed annoyance at* this.
>
> DEAN

or

> *The second operation was a reassessment, which I ordered in 1970, of the adequacy of internal security measures.* This resulted in a plan and a directive to strengthen our intelligence operations. They *were protested by Mr. Hoover, and as a result of his protest* they *were not put into effect.*
>
> NIXON

The "operation" resulted in a plan? The "reassessment" resulted in a plan? The "adequacy of internal security measures" resulted in a plan? And what did Mr. Hoover protest? "This"? "Internal security measures"? The "directive"? You see how valuable vague pronoun references can be.

Well, it was very simple. We don't need this. *I am tired of hearing of* it. *Out. Let's not discuss it any further. In my opinion,* it *was just as clear as* that.
MITCHELL

By the skillful use of "it" with no known antecedent, Mitchell has been known to talk for hours, even days, without revealing one particle of information.

The ultimate in DCD is the incomplete sentence, combining as it does evasiveness, obscurity, and incorrectness. Consider the following examples:

Discovering information about a person who I had been told by Mr. Hunt was a traitor, who was passing, he or his associates, to a foreign embassy.
BARKER

And this morning, after assessing all of the considerations and the outcome of those actions, which were not preplanned, not desired and, indeed, I think probably not very well visualized on Friday morning by all participants—this is the setting in which the President entered the Oval Office this morning.
GENERAL HAIG

When your honor went into the question of intent and motive and you were talking about that a minute ago, what I am telling you is that what they are trying to prove the motive is.

CHARLES MORGAN, JR.

So you can see that with misused words, bad prepositional phrases, erroneous reflexives, lack of subject-verb agreement, incomplete sentences, and vague pronoun references the government officials who write in the D.C. Dialect guarantee the protection of all top secret memos and documents. Obviously, there is no longer any danger to national security from "leaks" of secret material, because no one—including the most fluent English-speaking spies can possibly understand any of it.

Lesson 8:

Be Faddish

This memorandum addresses the matter of how we can maximize the fact of our incumbency in dealing with persons known to be active in their opposition to our administration.

JOHN DEAN

Fill your vocabulary with the latest "in" words. DCD speakers are always on the lookout for different and "innovative" words and meanings. Government officials are nothing if not abreast of the times, and you must be too. You must haunt the bookstores for the latest descriptive dictionaries so you can keep up with the most recent accepted usage. Whatever the newest words—however tacky and ungainly—use them in your speech, and you will thereby proclaim yourself a modern and fashionable member of the in-group. If DCD speakers choose to ignore George Orwell's warning that the English language "becomes ugly and inaccurate because our thoughts are foolish," then you can too. After all, what did Orwell know?

One of the most popular fad words in DCD is "fund." Instead of using the word in the traditional way as in "trust fund," DCD people always use it in place of "money" and "paid for." Use it as a noun, a verb, or whatever, and your speech will take on a modish tone. Note the effect:

funding was not available

to fund the project

the overall amount of funding

providing funding assistance

funded the campaign

assist them with funding

Another "now" word is "thrust." Instead of saying "direction," say "... the thrust of your question," as Robert Mardian does, or say "I think that was the thrust of the statement," as John Mitchell does. Instead of saying "impetus," say "... go forward with a full thrust," as Mr. Nixon says.

It may come as a surprise to a lot of farmers, but the word "implement" no longer simply means tool, but is now a verb meaning "to carry out," or "to put into effect" (or as DCD experts would say, "effectuate"). It's one of the favorite verbs in DCD, so you must use it often.

I want to emphasize that if you implement your plans as we discussed, the President will adequately recognize you.

MARUMOTO memo

... I was told to see what I could do to get the first step implemented.

DEAN

... the implementation of this reporting channel ...

LAIRD

Consider the value of the suffix "ize": by adding these three little letters to a word you come up with a really faddish sound. "Maximum" is a case in point. As it stands it is simply a dull, traditional word derived from mathematics, but add "ize" to the root, turn the word into a verb, and get a brand new "ugly."

... the opposition was attempting to maximize this.

GENERAL WALTERS

... were making a lot of noise and the Democrats were trying to maximize it.

RICHARD HELMS

"Lifestyle," "viable," "ongoing," and "innovative" are also quite chic these days. To practice using them, update the following old-fashioned sentences with these four words.

1. The oil shortage has affected our lives.
2. He suggested a workable solution.
3. A continuing effort is being made to discover the truth.
4. They proposed a new program for the schools.

To enhance your image among the VIPs, always substitute the popular word "indicate" for "say" or "tell."

Mr. Bittman indicated to me that he had received the affidavit. . . . I indicated I had no difficulty with it whatever.

HUNT

Mr. Liddy came in and indicated that he had had trouble the night before, that they tried to do a survey of the McGovern headquarters and Mr. Liddy indicated that to assist this he had shot a light out.

MAGRUDER

After I had recovered from the shock, I indicated, "Well, you go ahead and try to reach him and I will try to reach him as well."

CAULFIELD

Sometimes, though, the use of "indicate" can get out of hand, as in this exchange between Senator Weicker and Jeb Magruder:

WEICKER: *Who was he talking about when he indicated that you would not be indicted?*

MAGRUDER: *You were indicating whether there was any influence. My indication from Mr. Dean was that they had no influence over the U.S. attorney.*

And to maintain your popularity in the DCD smart set, discard those moldy-oldies, "workable," "usable," and "practical," and dress up your vocabulary with the more stylish "viable."

A viable presidency is a cornerstone of world security.
HAIG

We never found a scintilla of viable evidence indicating that these demonstrators were part of a master plan.
DEAN

In hindsight, I would think that would have been a very viable thing to do.
MITCHELL

I think we disagree as to whether or not that is a viable.
EHRLICHMAN

80

So much "bugging" goes on nowadays that another fashionable word, "bugger," has entered the language to mean "one who installs 'bugs.' " This term will no doubt lead to a great deal of confusion, because in print the word can easily be mistaken for the old children's favorite, "bugger"—pronounced to rhyme with "sugar." And the word may horrify the British, who will think that Washington, D.C. is crawling with sodomists!

The most ubiquitous new word, although it is actually an old advertising term, is "media." Everybody uses it—or almost everybody. You must never use the word "news" by itself anymore, but do as Mr. Nixon does and say "news media." If you slip up and use "news" alone, you'll be thought a hick, since hicks are the only people in the nation now who don't say "media"—and everybody knows that hicks can't learn DCD.

The recent shift of meaning of the word "clout" might also cause the backward to be confused. An associate of Earl Butz was heard to say of him that "He just used up all the clout he had and gave in on beef." Those who know the older meanings of "clout" may think it odd that the Secretary of Agriculture has used up all his clotted cream, or patches, or blows with the fist. And they might be even more confused by this statement by an "inside White House source," commenting on Melvin Laird:

His clout will be felt all over the White House.

We hasten to assure the language laggards that the

81

statement does not mean that the White House is full of clout-feelers, nor does it mean that Mr. Laird intended to punch everybody in the White House in the nose. "Clout" is now merely a faddish substitute for that dull old word "influence."

To help update your speech, study the attractive words and phrases in these modish sentences.

I think you and John could be negotiated out.

MITCHELL

The big man involved stature-wise *was the attorney general, Mr. John Mitchell.*

HUNT

The liquidity *of some enterprises has been called into question.*

BURNS

I do not think I ever knew with any particularity *why.*

EHRLICHMAN

It is a negative *in setting forth general information involving questions.*

NIXON

Before the public eye—the focus *of attention is on the* negatives *of the administration.*

HALDEMAN

. . . with a valet to shine Nixon's shoes and a maid to do the housework, Nixon was thus freed for transition activities.

ASH

So get in the forefront of the "innovators." Rush to the head of the line that is trampling on the old words and meanings. After all, it's only a matter of time until *all* the dictionaries catch up with the D.C. Dialect and accept such engaging words as "hypothecate," "definitional," "pendency," "capsulized," and "backgrounder."

Lesson 9:

Be Serious

There is no question that the heavy part of our rise is behind us.

EARL BUTZ

Keep in mind that the D.C. Dialect is no laughing matter. Like Victorian poets, people who speak the dialect are dedicated to high seriousness; in fact, there is absolutely no place in DCD for levity. People who laugh are suspected of having ulterior motives and warped ideologies. Wisecracks are permitted in DCD, but not humor, and there is a significant difference, as you shall see.

The following are examples of DCD wisecracks. The fact that there are only three will give you some idea of their paucity in the dialect.

I think he's got butterfly screws behind his ears which he turns occasionally to get rid of the wrinkles.

SEN. JOHN TOWER

I've always been scared of anybody who says he is a country lawyer.

WILSON

HALDEMAN: *Gray, the symbol of wisdom today and future counsel for tomorrow.*

DEAN: *Maybe someone will shoot him.*

Of course you should be able to *make up* "jokes" like the above without our help. What we must instruct you on is *unintentional* humor, which can catch you with your dialect down, so to speak. Even the very best of DCD speakers slip and say funny things now and then—sometimes at the most awkward times. We shall give you several examples of these unfortunate lapses so you can guard against similar gaffes:

As most lawyers, I'm human.

MARDIAN

I don't want to be dragged by the rear into a chaotic presentation of this.

SAMUEL DASH

. . . the second operation was on Mr. Hoover's death.

BARKER

85

He needs and wants information on supporters.

EHRLICHMAN

It was not an in-house White House unit.

HALDEMAN

We responded down to the floor above.

a police officer

The laundry's in the ice-box.

ANTHONY ULASEWICZ

Mr. Nixon, speaking of the publication of the Pentagon Papers, unwittingly made a funny by revealing ignorance in high places.

Not until a few hours before publication did any responsible government official know that they had been stolen. Most officials did not know they existed. No senior official of the government had read them or knew with certainty what they contained.

This remarkable statement makes several facts perfectly clear:

1. Only *irresponsible* government officials are informed of important thefts.

2. Most government officials know little of government papers.
3. No senior officials read important government papers.
4. No senior officials know for sure what is in top secret papers.

Nor are generals immune to linguistic lapses, as you can see from this curious comment from the Pentagon:

War does a great many things to the Army.

And Senator Howard Baker poses an unusual dilemma when he asks about McCord's reputation:

. . . would you say his reputation as a human being, a man, and as an employee . . .

How does one go about compiling records of someone's reputation as a human being? "He's a human being, all right. He has all the characteristics of homo sapiens." "As a human being, McCord ranks right up there with the best. He never monkeys around." Some affidavits along these lines might serve, but the question remains a sticky one.

Mr. Kleindienst also commits a serious faux pas; he bestows God-like power on Mr. Nixon by saying that he "caused the memos to be Xeroxed."

Not only is high seriousness mortally wounded by unintentional funnies, but decorum is often injured as well. Some comments by speakers of the dialect can only be classified as suggestive. For instance, right in the middle of serious business about presidential tapes, Andrew Butterfield suggests that someone ought to do something about the storage problem in order "to get a leg up on these tapes."

These next comments also come dangerously close to being risqué.

There are people who are involved in the campaign who have a tremendous exposure . . .

However, I would like to broaden my exposure to the world to some extent by possibly going in other directions.

AGNEW

Occasionally a few unfortunate words make something suggestive out of a perfectly serious remark:

My preoccupation during these months was to keep the agency at a distance. When I saw these feelers being made, it was suppository, "Do you suppose these things could be done?"

HELMS

Suppositories made of "feelers"? Pharmacists around the country must have consulted their U.S. Pharmacopeia, and doctors must have been aghast.

The word "audit" often poses problems for the unwary speaker of the dialect. Consider these rather indelicate remarks:

> *There is an audit function also.*
>
> JAMES T. LYNN

> *We have been unable to stimulate audits of persons who should be audited.*
>
> White House memo

> *I think he was able to accomplish an audit on the individual.*
>
> DEAN

Would you want your audit "stimulated," or would you want an audit "accomplished" on you?

Sometimes the unintentional "funnies" in the dialect bring to mind science fiction novels and horror stories. When Strachan says

> *I can't picture in my mind the capability in my prior office.*

one wonders what a "capability" looks like, and whether it

is still there lurking or shuffling like some mythological beast kept secretly chained, a pitiful creature who exists on tapes and memoranda? All we know for sure is that the creature lives caged in a "prior office." (Perhaps a "prior office" *is* a type of cage.) And one of Senator Weicker's remarks shows that Strachan is not the only official in Washington who keeps a "capability":

It is true, then, that you acquired a beefed-up litigating capability.

Yet another science fiction image is conjured up in this ominous observation:

There has, however, been some loose talk of an impending credit crunch . . .

BURNS

"Credit crunch" sounds for all the world like a giant chunk of peanut brittle, hunkering on the horizon. And Mr. Nixon mentions "a backward-looking obsession," which suggests a nostalgic beast of some sort. "Capabilities" in offices, "obsessions" that can look back, and "impending credit crunches" may be what Mitchell is referring to when he talks of the "White House horrors."

It is hard to imagine what could have spawned this amazing picture:

Of course, every time you have a freeze there is char-

acteristically a short post freeze bubble. I think it is fair
to say that the rules for Phase 4 will be designed in such
a way as to minimize that bubble. We will also try to
minimize that potential bubble in administrating the
freeze.

JAMES W. MCLANE

Mr. McLane seems to believe that there is such a thing as a
"short" bubble that can be "minimized," which in turn is
only a "potential" bubble that has something to do with a
"freeze."

Mrs. Anne Armstrong, one of the few female speakers
of the dialect, matches wits (or wit) with the men when she
accidentally drops this gem.

. . . people can keep calm and have patience and wait
for this bulge to even out.

Many speakers of the D.C. Dialect "speak" to abstrac-
tions and inanimate objects. Haldeman's appointment as
Lord High Executioner for Leaks, however, may have
unhinged his reason, because he claims that "The Chairman spoke to the story . . ." Now in these trying times of
tapes and tapped telephones it would not be unusual for
the Chairman to speak to a wall, or a desk, but it is
far-fetched to suppose that he would speak to a *story*. Mr.
Agnew comes right out and admits that he spends a lot of
time talking to abstract thought, of all things!

91

I probably talk more to philosophy than anyone in politics today . . .

References to unusual foods often appear in the accidental funnies of the dialect, some of which also have a "science fiction" ring to them and are a bit difficult to understand.

We will keep tabs on examples of partisan press treatment and feed them into the Vice President (and Cabinet officers on the stump) on a regular basis.
HIGBY memo

Who in the world would want to stand on a stump and eat tabs as a steady diet? But Mr. Butz refers to foods in a more appealing way, thank goodness:

We're coming into the heavy barbecue season.

We must assume that Mr. Butz (having worked so long with agriculture) is wise in the ways of food, and that heavy barbecue is to be preferred to light barbecue.

Some DCD funnies seem to be riddles. When General Walters says "I stand on my own recollection," we naturally wonder how he could possible do such a thing. But the General's surefootedness is nothing compared to Ehrlichman's:

92

I stand flatly on all four corners of that conversation.

Quite a trick. Of course if the conversation is small it might not be too difficult, although it is surprising that anyone would admit to having flat feet. But then Ehrlichman admits to having a "what-not" on his face, so perhaps we shouldn't be surprised.

> *. . . The anguish, disbelief, and what-not on my face, when he told me I was indictable.*

Or how about this singular assertion by Mr. Mitchell, who claims he has never done anything "mentally wrong"?

> *The only thing I did was to try to get the President re-elected. I never did anything mentally or morally wrong.*

Linguistic riddles can be damagingly funny, but mixed metaphors can be devastating, so avoid them at all costs. The high seriousness of DCD can't stand too many assaults like the one that Haldeman makes when he quotes Dean as saying

> *. . . draw the wagons around the White House and let the chips fall where they may.*

93

Lesson 10:

Be Unintelligible

As I understand the sequence of events when this thrashing around was involved, occurred, involving everybody from the President of the United States and the chairman of this committee and everybody on down the line as anybody they could think of to name, Mr. Parkinson.

JOHN MITCHELL

Polish your dialect to a fine point of unintelligibility for private conversations. DCD people *do* speak to one another in private, and you must pass the test of intimate conversation with your peers. Certain rules do not fully apply to private speech, however; for example, you may delete a portion of pomposity, a bit of repetition, and a certain amount of evasiveness. And some rules are simply suspended—you may spice private conversations with expletives, descriptive characterizations, and even interjections! Lest you relax your guard too much, though, we must warn you that the rules governing incorrectness, awkwardness, obscurity and seriousness remain in force.

The chief consideration to keep in mind in order to be unintelligible is that you must never speak *logically*—non sequiturs are the order of the day. When one of your Very Important Colleagues addresses you, reply with some remark that is totally off the subject. He will not be surprised; he is not listening to you anyway, and will reply to your remark with a non sequitur of his own. The following examples of professional non sequiturs (and all other quotes in this lesson) are taken from the White House transcripts, a truly invaluable collection of DCD private speech.

NIXON: *They wanted it for that purpose. And the question is what you thought it was. And then again they'll say that they don't believe you. It'll get down to that.*

ROGERS: *Dash, etc.*

NIXON: *There again, though, course they have a route to this. LaRue. He broke down and cried, I guess.*

EHRLICHMAN: *That's a-right. Are you going to have spaghetti tonight?*

ROGERS: *Spaghetti and singing Toscanni.*

NIXON: *Well, Bill. You go ahead. I'll—let them go home. It's possible we may ask your advice tomorrow with all—*

ROGERS: *I have reason to feel good that you got John Wilson.*

If the foregoing seems slightly overwhelming at first glance, take heart. Speaking illogically is not so much an art as a skill—one that can be learned. As preparation, we urge you to see several dramas of the absurd, read a few textbooks on abnormal psychology, and go to as many Marx Brothers' movies as possible.

Note that as many as five seasoned dialect speakers can take part in a non sequitur conversation with ease. Try it out on your friends at the next Tupperware party or Rotary Club meeting.

NIXON: *But some of the questions look big hanging out publicly or privately.*

DEAN: *What it is doing, Mr. President, is getting you up above and away from it. That is the most important thing.*

NIXON: *Oh, I know. I suggested that the other day and they all came down negative on it. Now what has changed their minds?*

DEAN: *Lack of candidate or a body.*

HALDEMAN: *(Laughter)*

MITCHELL: *(Inaudible) We went down every alley.*

NIXON: *I feel that at a very minimum we've got to have this statement. Let's look at it. I don't know what it—where in the hell is it—if it opens up doors, it opens up doors—you know.*

HALDEMAN: *John says he is sorry he sent those burglars in there—and that helps a lot.*

NIXON: *That's right.*

EHRLICHMAN: *You are very welcome, sir.*

Here are some short non sequiturs for you to practice on in case you don't have more than two or three people to talk to:

NIXON: *Come in. As, like all things, some substance, some falsity.*

PETERSEN: *Ah. Last Monday Charlie Shaffer was in the office, and a continuation of the negotiations.*

NIXON: *Now Ron, brainstorm that for us—what do you think—that's—*

Ziegler: *First of all, the way to do this, and I think we should do this, but the way to do this—the feeling that something is happening in town and you (inaudible).*

HALDEMAN: *Yes. I have this brother-in-law in school—*

DEAN: *He wants a wild scenario.*

HALDEMAN: *My friend is writing a play, and he wants to see how—*

DEAN: *It bothers me to do anything further now, sir, when Hunt is our real unknown.*

The next quotes reveal the relaxation of the impersonal rules in private speech. First names are allowed, but one mustn't go too far with them, and it is wise to revert to surnames. Note the amount of intimacy allowed.

KLEINDIENST: *Hi, John.*

EHRLICHMAN: *Hi, General. How are you?*

KLEINDIENST: *How was the golf?*

EHRLICHMAN: *Half good and half bad.*

98

KLEINDIENST: *Who else does Magruder implicate besides himself and Mitchell?*

Ehrlichman: *Dean, LaRue, Mardian, Porter.*

Of course, people accustomed to using the impersonal in public often become confused when they revert to Christian names, so you must be very careful.

HALDEMAN: *It went to Baroody which was the—*

EHRLICHMAN: *Bill or another Baroody?*

HALDEMAN: *No, Sam or Charlie.*

EHRLICHMAN: *Sam.*

HALDEMAN: *Or Edgar or somebody. One of the others.*

NIXON: *You remember the meeting we had when I told that group of clowns we had around there. Renchburg and that group. What's his name?*

EHRLICHMAN: *Rehnquist.*

NIXON: *Yeah. Rehnquist.*

The real fun of private conversations lies in the freedom to speak your mind about others without being hampered by the rules governing public speech. Your imagination can take flights of fancy as you deftly characterize friends and enemies.

Bobby was a ruthless (characterization omitted).

They say no civilized (characterization deleted) informs.

(expletives deleted) Colson's got (characterization deleted).

There is no problem with Sullivan. He is a valuable man. Now would the FBI turn on him (characterization deleted).

NIXON

The most professional DCD speakers tape their private conversations because of their unselfish wish to record their Very Important Thoughts for posterity. If you wish to emulate these officials, you must be prepared to spend money equipping home, office, car, restaurants, drugstores, laundromats, post offices, doctor's offices, schools, etc. with "voice-activating" tapes which will capture your most intimate conversations. Lest you be put off by the cost of such equipment, we hasten to add that defective, second-hand equipment is much to be preferred. The shoddier the machines, the less likelihood that the tapes will be intelligible should they fall into the hands of your enemies. Note the following, which cleverly yields its meaning only to those DCD friends "in the know."

> *No—no. I'm putting him up. The only thing I would say is that—to him—I would say that as President's counsel (unintelligible) executive (unintelligible) and all that—(expletive removed) I wouldn't even (unintelligible).*
>
> NIXON

Intimate talk is great good fun, of course, and is relatively easy to learn, but again we must caution you. DCD speakers can spot a phony—a speaker of English—quickly by his indiscreet use of proper logic and order, but even quicker by his use of appropriate imagery. Again we strongly urge you to study old Marx Brothers' movies to improve your grasp of the absurd and ridiculous. Keep in mind the enormous premium placed on unintelligibility by DCD folk, and lard your private speech with strange sayings like these:

> *. . . you are taking away a prosecutorial tool from them.*

> *I just don't see how we can minimize that man.*
>
> PETERSEN

> *. . . they better watch their damned cotton picking faces.*

101

. . . there's a difference between actors and noticees.

What stroke have you got with Magruder?
                    NIXON

*I am sure he will rationalize himself into a fable that
hangs together.*
                    EHRLICHMAN

The master of this sort of thing, however, is John Dean,
who never fails to impress with his sense of the absurd.
You can learn a lot by studying his interesting imagery.

*Judge Ritchie . . . has made several entrees off the
bench—*

*. . . as you all know, I was all over this thing like a wet
blanket.*

I think he helped to get the thing off the dime.

You have to wash the money.

*He can go in and stonewall . . . Stonewall, with lots of
noises that we are always willing to cooperate . . .*
                    DEAN

Sometimes private conversations in the dialect contain
literary allusions. For instance, when Ehrlichman says,

"Colson called and says you've got an ass at your bosom over there," he is obviously referring to the relationship between Bottom and Titania in *A Midsummer Night's Dream*. And judging by the following, John Dean and Henry Petersen are students of English Renaissance assassinations:

That may be his guts poker in the course of negotiations.

He told me that he had been designated . . . to accumulate all these facts . . . and that you'd be clearing his ass out if he didn't have it.

PETERSEN

. . . the people are starting to protect their own behind.

DEAN

Clearly, these remarks are references to the unfortunate fate of the king in Marlowe's *Edward II*.

Another popular subject in private conversation is medicine. Phrases such as "extensive hemorrhages," "a total rupture with the Director," "massive leaks," and "suck up the contents and then . . . regurgitate them," show DCD preoccupation with bodily functions and illnesses, as do the following comments:

We've got to prick the boil and take the heat . . .

NIXON

103

I think he was pressed up against the wall, he's seen the early-morning crisis pass, and now he's had resurgence.

PETERSEN

There is particular concern about contagious diseases —you might brush up your knowledge of preventive medicine so you'll be able to keep up with the other speakers.

I don't want to immunize John Dean . . .

We can't very well immunize him and put him head to head against a witness who is going to beat him.

PETERSEN

Why the hell did we give him immunization and not the poor damn Cubans?

NIXON

The poor Cubans may have typhoid or cholera by now!

In private, VIPs can relax and let their conversational hair down. In the following exchange, the speakers lightheartedly play with a current term of the youth culture, "hang out." As you can see, these Washington officials are completely at ease at any linguistic level, but they add just a touch of indelicacy and a small flourish of repetition to mark the conversation as genuine DCD:

104

NIXON: *Do you think we want to go this route now? Let it hang out so to speak?*

DEAN: *Well, it isn't really that—*

HALDEMAN: *It's a limited hang out.*

DEAN: *It is a limited hang out. It's not an absolute hang out.*

NIXON: *But some of the questions look big hanging out publicly or privately.*

So prepare yourself. Stock up on lusty literary allusions, motley metaphors, nimble non sequiturs, abstruse absurdities and salacious slang. And when next you find yourself eyeball to eyeball with an authentic, DCD-speaking VIP, you'll be ready. He'll take you for a Very Important Person, and your fortune in Washington will be assured!

Chapter Three

The Imagery Crisis:
Figures of Speech in DCD

The President sufficiently stimulated Mr. Hoover...
JOHN EHRLICHMAN

If you have mastered all the lessons of the D.C. Dialect, you are ready to plunge into the figures of speech. But a word of caution—there is a crisis of sorts in the dialect: There is a shortage of images! The problem is that almost all the figurative language of DCD is derived from the four occupations that are the background of most speakers of the dialect: the military, the law, business and sports. Everyone knows that these sources have been mined for figures of speech almost to the point of exhaustion in our times, so the difficulty is to use these sources inventively as DCD people do.

Military metaphors are relatively easy to come by, but you mustn't use them in the ways ordinary people do—none of that "War is hell" stuff. Instead you must show a lot of imagination as these speakers do:

Dean out there is a loose cannon.

*This is a war. We take a few shots and it will be over.
We will give them a few shots and it will be over.*

*I think if they have to have this blunderbuss in the
public arena then this is all it is.*

NIXON

. . . to mobilize the Republican troops . . .

*Buchanan, in response to his attack, argues quite
strongly the point that the attacks should always turn
to the positive side. He argues that this is wrong, and
the attacks should stay on the negative side. Do not try
to weave in also positive points. That there should be an
attack program that is purely attack.*

Ehrlichman shot down that thought.

HALDEMAN

I knew what my marching orders were.

EHRLICHMAN

He was beginning to protect his flanks.

DEAN

If you like, you can switch to naval imagery, and come up
with unusual figures of speech like these:

The ship is leaving the dock and you'd better get aboard.

"inside source"

. . . the name of Mr. Hunt surfaced in connection with Watergate . . .

KLEINDIENST

I know that all Republicans will join me in welcoming Mr. Connally aboard.

AGNEW

I can assure you that you don't need to worry about my getting seasick or jumping ship. It is the captain's job to bring the ship to port. I am going to stay at the helm until we bring it into port.

NIXON (addressing the Seafarers' International Union)

It takes considerable brainpower to come up with uncommon imagery like this, so you'll probably have to practice quite a bit at first.

You don't need to worry about figurative language based on the law, because there's not really very much of it. Sometimes a felicitous metaphor like Dean's "They will have intense civil discovery," or Mardian's "potential target defendants" becomes popular with the DCD crowd, but for the most part all you need to do is scatter legal terminology throughout your speech, and the overall effect will be much like imagery—your tone will be heavy with connotations of brief cases, gavels, juries, and other paraphernalia of jurisprudence.

Business figures of speech, however, abound in DCD, and if you learn how to create them you can give the impression that you are also an expert in public relations, or real estate, or advertising, or computer programming. Notice how expert these speakers sound:

> *. . . welcomed the aveune of communication. I'm not going to foreclose the possibility . . .*
> AGNEW

> *They are "net worthing" him to death . . .*
> an Agnew financial aide

> *Your profile maintains Mr. Mitchell is your sponsor.*
> SENATOR WEICKER

> *We must lower the profile of the White House staff.*
> "a senior official"

Haldeman's use of "zero-defect system" to mean perfection shows the strong emphasis in the dialect on corporate language.

> *I would hope to be a part of the process by which programs are finalized—to have an input in their formulation.*
>
> GERALD FORD

> *I was certain Mitchell wasn't about to be programmed into being a fund-raiser . . .*
>
> MOORE

> *I didn't understand that he was the button-pusher.*
>
> KALMBACH

> *I only had a final sign-off on the end product.*
>
> HALDEMAN

It will greatly increase your chances of breaking into DCD society if you think and speak of people in terms of machines—things that can and should be manipulated. Very Important People, after all, do not have the time to *persuade* others; it is so much quicker to punch buttons and *direct* them.

> *Mitchell requested Dean to activate Kalmbach.*
>
> PETERSEN

110

. . . he dealt with people telephonically.

DEAN

Hunt and Liddy went off my screen.

EHRLICHMAN

If you are not a sports fan, it would be wise to become one immediately so you can fill your speech with sports imagery. (Which sport you pursue is not important, except that you must attend all Washington Redskin football games, which, admittedly, will work a hardship on you if you live in Utah.) Once you become a fan—not a participant, just a fan—you will be able to come up with such imaginative phrases as "touched base," and "a game plan to harass our political enemies." Study the following images from the experts and notice the skillful ways that sports metaphors can be used. Consider these choice "ball" metaphors, for example:

You know he was president for five and a half years, and I guess people dropped the ball along the way.

ZIEGLER

That's what the Army has to focus on. You've got to put the time and the effort into training, into discipline, into organization, into techniques. The Army must never take its eye off that ball.

"a Pentagon spokesman"

111

. . . throw the ball back in Dean's court . . .
Anon.

He is playing hard ball. He wouldn't play hard ball unless he were pretty confident that he could cause an awful lot of grief.

. . . wasn't playing ball in the cover-up plot.

DEAN

DCD sports imagery is heavy on "team play" and "game plans."

I think I would try to be a team player.

FORD

I was double-teamed.

ROBERT FINCH

He said I was fouling up the game plan.

CAULFIELD

When did you suspect that Mr. Dean got off your team?

SEN. DANIEL INOUYE

There is a shortage of baseball imagery in the dialect, possibly because the Washington Senators are now the

112

Texas Rangers. Mr. Agnew, however, seems to be a dedicated fan, and often comes up with baseball references like

. . . I've touched base also in Saudi Arabia and Kuwait.

Most DCD fans, however, prefer football, as you can tell from these unique metaphors:

I know that the Congress is usually a last-quarter team. In that last quarter we have to score a lot of points.

NIXON

In the Monday morning quarterback field in what has developed into the circumstances that exist today . . .

MITCHELL

But the best DCD speaker for spots imagery is able to create extended metaphors that boggle the mind! When you can think up an analogy like this one you'll know you've arrived.

I only wish that I could take the entire United States into the locker room at halftime. It would be an opportunity to say that we have lost yards against the line drives of inflation and the end runs of energy shortages, and that we are not using all our players as well as we

might because there is too much unemployment. There would be no excuses about previous coaches and previous seasons. I would simply say that we must look not at the points we have lost but at the points we can gain. We have a winner.

FORD

There is some figurative speech not based on any of the foregoing sources which gives variety and spice to the dialect. Like all languages, DCD has its own sexual imagery—language which reveals the strong masculine bias of the dialect and which gives a robust and healthy tone to its speech patterns. Consider the following:

. . . a little feel of it that Dean had given me.

. . . had very guardedly and covertly advanced feelers to him which he rebuffed.

We think of this as more "puffing" than "stroking."

. . . a shortfalling performance.

EHRLICHMAN

I received a stroking call from the President . . .

Through Strachan, who was his tickler, he started pushing to get some information.

114

In fact that was one of our problems—the little pocket of women who worked for Maury Stans. There is no doubt that things would have sailed a lot smoother without that pack.

DEAN

We don't want to put a hard probability on it.

SIMON

I've been around this town; I'm not a virgin.

HAIG

There is also figurative language in the dialect which reveals amazing mental flights of fantasy. Note that these illuminating and often stunning images expose an imaginative and eccentric power once found only in science fiction literature.

the fruits of the tapes

some of the fruits of the bugging

HALDEMAN

He told me to shred the documents and deep-six the briefcase.

DEAN

flash alias documentation

115

notional pocket litter documentation

GENERAL WALTERS

Dean was salting the mine a little bit.

. . . spreading anecdotal tales across the landscape.

EHRLICHMAN

And these next figures of speech evoke the atmosphere of exciting horror movies:

[Gray is] hanging in the wind, and let him hang there. Let him twist—slowly, slowly.

EHRLICHMAN

We should let him bleed for a while at least.

BUTTERFIELD memo about
Fitzgerald's federal job

The briefcase contained electronic equipment, loose wires, Chap Sticks for your lips with wires coming out of them, and . . .

DEAN

Before leaving imagery, we must pause and pay tribute to those dialect speakers who create mixed metaphors. Mixed metaphors have the authority of arresting and

116

holding the listener's attention, a power that plain old common or garden variety metaphors often lack. DCD speakers, adept as they are at holding the attention of audiences, greatly value mixed metaphors for their captivating quality. No other dialect can boast such colorful figures of speech as the following:

Huntley will go out in a blaze of glory and we should attempt to pop his bubble.
HIGBY memo

There's no way that anyone can place in cement his opinions in advance of the issue crystallizing or formulating.
AGNEW

Blazing bubbles and crystallized cement, certainly interesting combinations, vie with the "texture" of Watergate in the following quotes. Mr. Nixon and Governor Wendell H. Ford seem at odds, Nixon holding out for a sort of hog-pen quality, and Governor Ford opting for a substance that both "sinks in" and "falls out."

. . . let others wallow in Watergate.
NIXON

I believe that Watergate is sinking in with the peo-

117

ple. . . . The fallout from Watergate is going to make
mountains out of molehills in politics.

GOVERNOR FORD

Mr. Agnew, in a most subtle metaphor, speaks of justice as a liquid which is capable of sin and salvation:

> *Lacking such safeguards, the Committee . . . can hardly hope to find the truth and can hardly fail to muddy the waters of justice beyond redemption . . .*

And L. Patrick Gray's audience must find him positively enchanting for such jolly (but admittedly difficult) suggestions as this:

> *I think you should tell John Wesley to stand awfully tight in the saddle.*

Mr. McCord does his bit for the imagery shortage by providing several images at one time—a sort of mixed bag of metaphors, as it were.

> *If the Watergate operation is laid at the CIA's feet where it does not belong, every tree in the forest will fall. . . . If they want it to blow, they are on the right course.*

But we must credit Henry Petersen with one of the most

unorthodox and arresting mixed metaphors; by pretending a shocking ignorance of the nature of minefields, he grabs the attention of his audience with the following:

I'm not a whore. I walked through a minefield and came out clean.

Now that you have studied some of the fine figures of speech in the dialect, you will have to admit that these speakers are nothing if not inventive and imaginative. But the imagery crisis remains. The four language currents that created DCD are simply not enough to provide the heavy load of imagery that will be needed in the next few years by public officials. We suggest, therefore, that in the interests of expanding the dialect, of providing it with more original metaphors, that you send your suggestions for new imagery to your favorite DCD speaker.

We know that you will want to have a part in improving the winningest speech of our times, and that your patriotic impulses will urge you to help expand this wonderful and useful new American speech, so we end this book with some additional suggestions that you can follow to help spread the D.C. Dialect to every speaker in the nation. Here they are:

1. Send your favorite quotes from DCD speakers to the Letters to the Editor column in your local newspaper. After all, you want to make people in your own community aware of fine phrases and turns of speech. Be sure

to give credit to the politician or official or executive who thought up the DCD-ism.

2. Send your favorite examples of DCD to the National Council of Teachers of English. If these silly critics of the dialect are bombarded with choice quotes, they will soon see the light and stop complaining and holding back progress. It's groups like the NCTE that always stand in the way of good old-fashioned American innovation.

3. Send your favorite quotes to the President of the United States. After all, his speech writers have more DCD to write than anybody else, and they're bound to be grateful for material, so pick it up wherever you find it and send it to them. If you're lucky, one of the White House speech writers will acknowledge your contribution and write you a thank-you note which you can frame and keep on your living room wall for years to come!

4. Send your favorite DCD quotes to local and national television and radio commentators and newscasters. Many of them need help, because they speak only rudimentary DCD or a shoddy imitation of it (and a few don't speak it at all!), and they'll be grateful for your contributions. Remember that it's hard for some people to learn a new dialect, because some don't have good ears for the finer points of speech and diction—so try not to condemn the announcers who are slow to pick up DCD, and, instead, try to help them with good sentences, words, and phrases.

5. If you're really serious about learning the D.C.

Dialect and getting ahead in the world, our last idea should be one for you! Have a button made that says DCD on it, and wear it proudly everywhere you go. Advertising is the American way, and display buttons are the "in" thing these days, so get in the swing and get out there with your symbol of the new, ongoing, taking-over language. Let everybody know that you're right up there with the VIPs in your effort to spread the greatest language yet invented! We end with a suggested DCD button, although you can make up your own if you like. Good luck in your studies and in your upward mobility!

I speak
DCD
Do you?

A Glossary of Selected Words and Phrases

Here's a helpful handbook full of felicitous phrases and dazzling diction, designed to hasten your mastery of DCD. Ordinary, commonplace English in the left column is translated into DCD on the right. Within weeks, with the aid of this glossary, you'll be able to make up your own sentences and expressions and have enough left over to send to Washington officials to help them expand this original dialect even further.

ENGLISH	D.C. DIALECT
alibi	deniability
approve/disapprove	sign off
before	1. prior to
	2. prior to the beginning of
begin	implement
Bill of Rights	restraints on intelligence collection
break-in	entry operation
building	facility
burglary	surreptitious entry
carry out	effectuate

ENGLISH	D.C. DIALECT
casing the joint	vulnerability and feasibility study
cause (v.)	effectuate
circumstance	situation
clot (medical)	inactive area of living tissue
comments	1. feedback
	2. input
commitment	firm commitment
concentrate	focus on
condition	situation
confidence	confidentiality
Congress	legislative facility
context	frame of reference
continuing	ongoing
courtroom	courtroom situation
cover-up	contain the situation
criminal conspiracy	game plan
death	terminal event
decrease	minimize
definitive	definitional
demand for money	a retieration of requests for keeping commitments, in the tradition of a bill collector
describe	characterize

ENGLISH	D.C. DIALECT
destroying evidence	shredding activity
	deep-six
diminish	minimize
direction	thrust
edifice	facility
energy crisis	energy problem
enlarge	maximize
exploit political power	maximize the fact of our incumbency
fact	1. firm fact
	2. hard fact
failing economy	lateral waffle
fear	degree of concern
finance (v.)	fund
financing (n.)	funding
fired	selected out
give money to someone	disburse to an individual
go-between	conduit
half truth	limited hang-out
happen	occur
home for spies	intelligence housing
hush money	increments in the form of currency
hypothesize	hypothecate
ideas	1. feedback
	2. input

124

ENGLISH	D.C. DIALECT
impetus	thrust
increase	maximize
influence	clout
intent	thurst
internal spies	domestic intelligence
invalid	inoperative
jet flight	ongoing diplomatic activity
kidnap	segregate out
know	be aware of
last to hand out hush money	ultimate distributees
lessen	minimize
life	lifestyle
magazines	news media
man	individual
memory	independent recollection
mention	indicate
Mexican Bank	laundry
microphone installer	bugger
money (n.)	funding
nagging fear	ongoing concern
narrow down	focus
national security	national security situation
networks	news media
new	innovative

ENGLISH	D.C. DIALECT
newspapers	news media
no's	negatives
not critical (medical)	sub-intensive
now	at this point in time
one lawyer, two ex-CIA agents, four Cuban-Americans	sophisticated political intelligence-gathering system
oriented	orientated
park	recreational facility
part	portion
pay (v.)	fund
pending	pendency
people	1. individuals
	2. personnel
perfection	zero-defect system
person	individual
pertaining to California	California-wise
phone call	telephonic information
plant (n.)	facility
plight	situation
point (n.)	thrust
point out	indicate
political sabotage	dirty tricks
position	situation
possible jail term	degree of involvement
power	clout

ENGLISH	D.C. DIALECT
practical	viable
predicament	situation
put into practice	implement
questions	1. interrogatories
	2. queries
rationing	end-use allocation
readers	readership
recession	energy-crisis spasm
remain as is	zero growth
remember	recollect
	test the chronology of one's knowledge
résumé	backgrounder
reveal	indicate
salary	compensation level
say	indicate
secrecy	confidentiality
separation of powers	executive immunity
signify	indicate
Smithsonian	museum facility
spies	1. intelligence community
	2. operatives
	3. plumbers
spying	intelligence activity
start	1. implement
	2. initiate

ENGLISH	D.C. DIALECT
state (n.)	situation
state (v.)	indicate
stature	stature-wise
subject	1. subject area
	2. subject matter
suggestions	1. feedback
	2. input
telephonic interception device	wiretap
television	1. communications media
	2. news media
tell	indicate
testify	put an end to an evidentiary chain
theft	bag job
then	at that point in time
time	time frame
to follow someone	visual surveillance
token inquiry	vigorous investigation
total immunity	executive privilege
use	utilize
useful	viable
wiretap	1. electronic surveillance
	2. telephonic interception device
won't work	counter-productive
workable	viable